I0820440

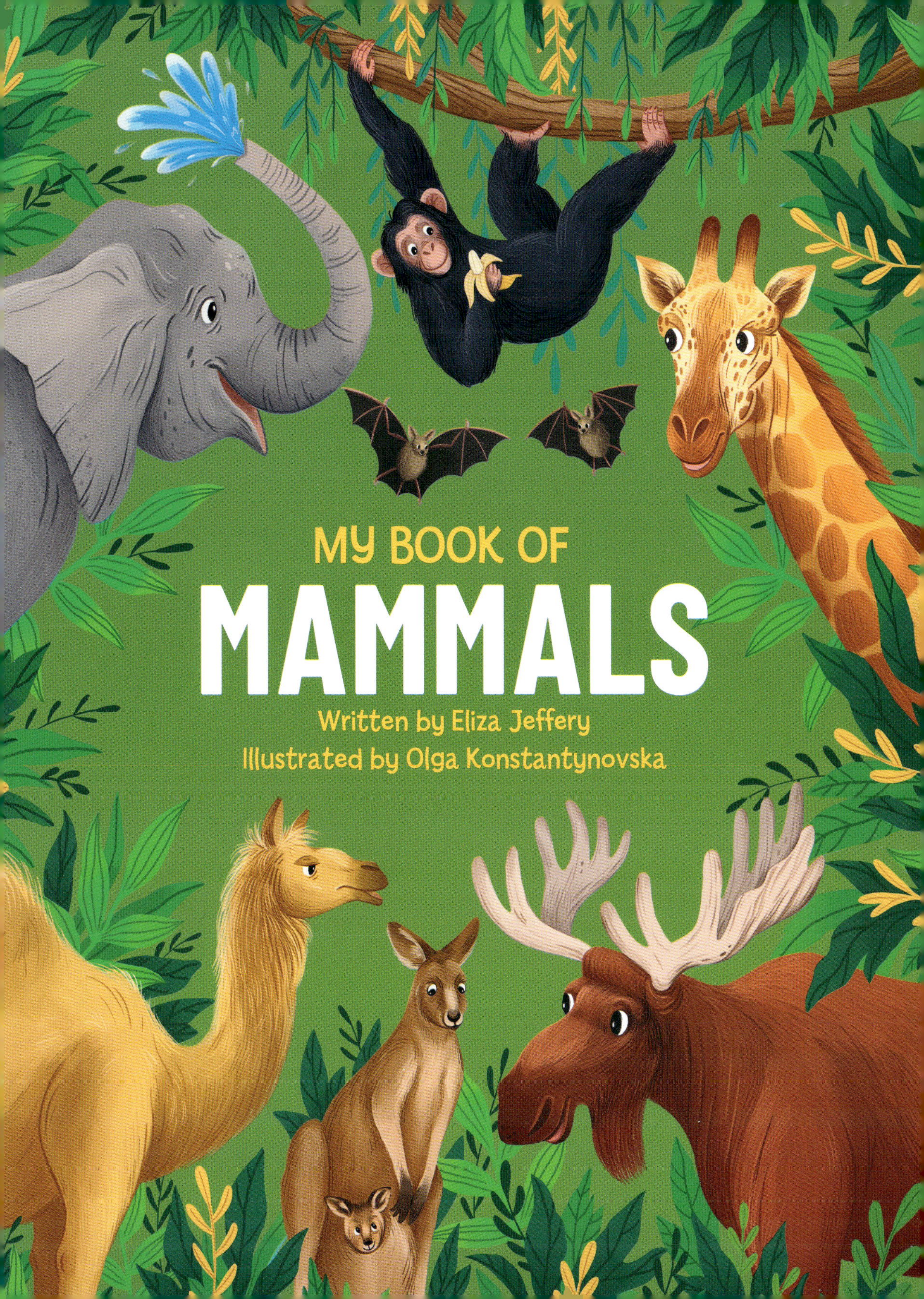
MY BOOK OF
MAMMALS
Written by Eliza Jeffery
Illustrated by Olga Konstantynovska

CONTENTS

First published in 2026 by Hungry Tomato Ltd
F15, Old Bakery Studios, Blewetts Wharf, Malpas Road, Truro, Cornwall,
TR1 1QH, UK.

A CIP catalog record for this book is available from the British Library.

ISBN 9781835694442

Manufactured in the USA

Discover more at
www.hungrytomato.com

Words in BOLD can be found in the glossary.

WHAT ARE MAMMALS?

Mammals are AMAZING!

You can find mammals in the sea, on land and even in the sky! There are around 6,000 different types of mammals. A mammal is an animal that has these four things:

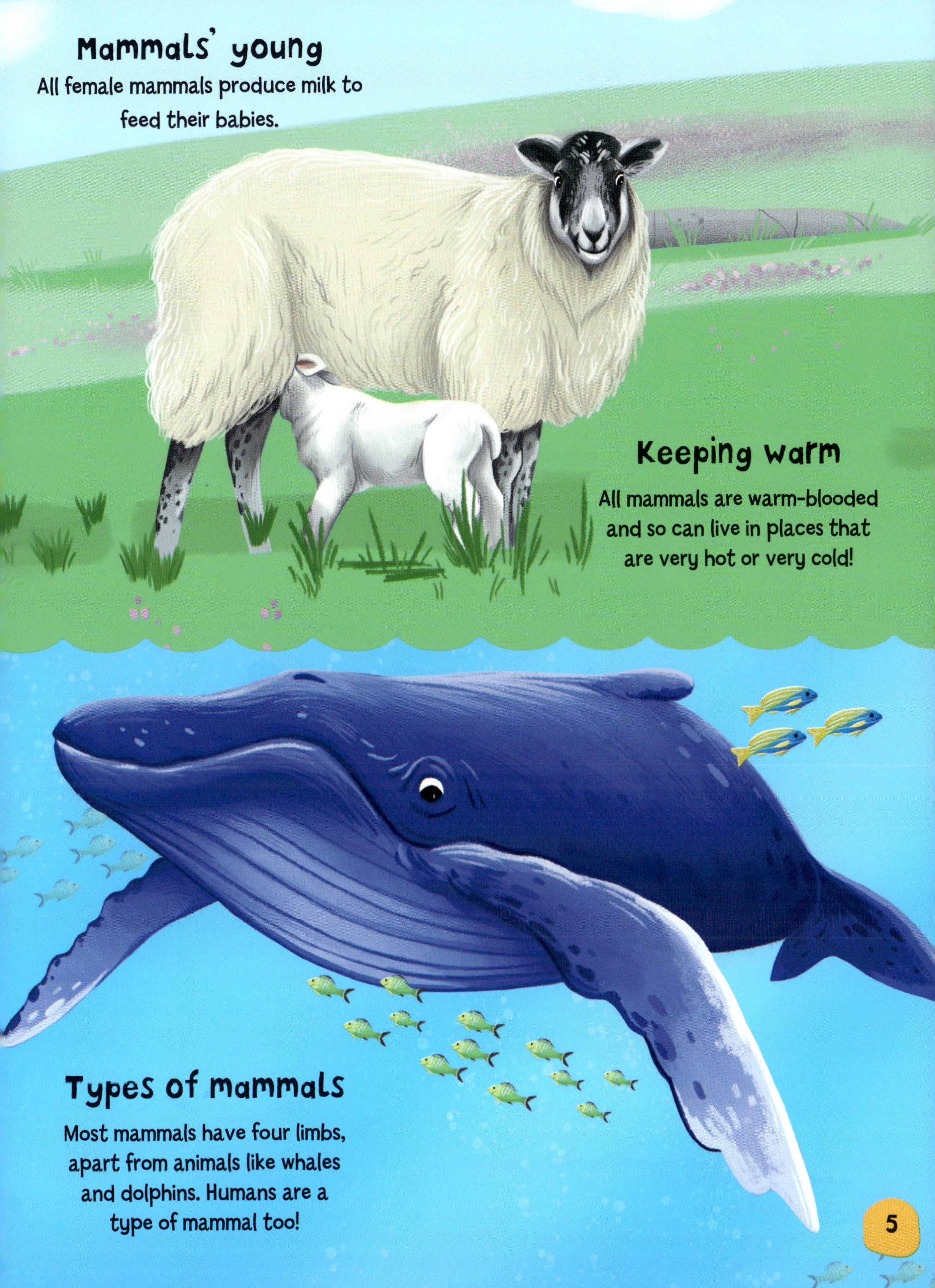

Mammals' young

All female mammals produce milk to feed their babies.

Keeping warm

All mammals are warm-blooded and so can live in places that are very hot or very cold!

Types of mammals

Most mammals have four limbs, apart from animals like whales and dolphins. Humans are a type of mammal too!

POLAR BEAR

Polar bears are the LARGEST CARNIVORES on land!

These wild animals are clever **predators**. They like to hunt on sea ice, waiting for seals to appear at the surface of the water, before pouncing!

Excellent sense of smell

Mothers and cubs have strong bonds.

They stay safe in snow dens.
DID YOU KNOW?
I am a... carnivore.
I eat... seals and fish.
My babies are called... cubs.
I can be found... in the Arctic.

GIRAFFE

Giraffes are the TALLEST MAMMALS!

Giraffes are most well known for their long necks. They are peaceful animals that spend most of their time **grazing**. They live in groups called corps or towers.

Long tongue to grab branches
DID YOU KNOW?
I am a... **herbivore.**
I eat... leaves, twigs and fruit.
My babies are called... calves.
I can be found... in Africa.

BLUE WHALE

Whales are the BIGGEST MAMMALS in the world!

Blue whales can be as long as three school buses! They have smooth, rubbery skin and slender bodies for gliding through the water. They come up to the surface to breathe air.

Blowhole to breathe air
Flippers and tail for **steering**
DID YOU KNOW?
I am a... carnivore.
I eat... krill, plankton and other mammals!
My babies are called... calves.
I can be found... in every ocean, except the Arctic.

LION

Lions are STRONG and have a POWERFUL ROAR!

A lion is one of the biggest cats in the world. Males are in charge of looking after the cubs while females are out hunting for **prey**. Newborn cubs have light spots on their fur.

DID YOU KNOW?

I am a... carnivore.

I eat... large animals, like zebra and wildebeest.

My babies are called... cubs.

I can be found... in Africa.

BAT

Bats are the only mammals in the world that can FLY!

Bats are **nocturnal** animals and sleep upside down so they can fly away quickly from predators. Bats are very sociable animals and live in big groups called colonies.

DID YOU KNOW?
I am an... **omnivore.**
I eat... fruit, insects and small rodents.
My babies are called... pups.
I can be found... almost everywhere!
Thin wings make flying easy.

KANGAROO

A kangaroo can leap up to 30 feet (9 meters) in the air WITH ONE BOUNCE!

Kangaroos live together in groups called troops. Male kangaroos fight using their own style of boxing to decide who the leader is.

Powerful
back legs
Long tail
for balance

ELEPHANT

Elephants are the HEAVIEST LAND MAMMALS!

An elephant can weigh up to 15,000 pounds (7,000 kilograms)! They live in groups called herds that are led by female elephants. Elephants are very sociable and create strong family bonds with each other that last a lifetime.

Calves hold onto their mother's tail to stay safe.

Long trunk for smelling, drinking and picking up food

The **tusks** are actually huge teeth that stick out of an elephant's mouth.

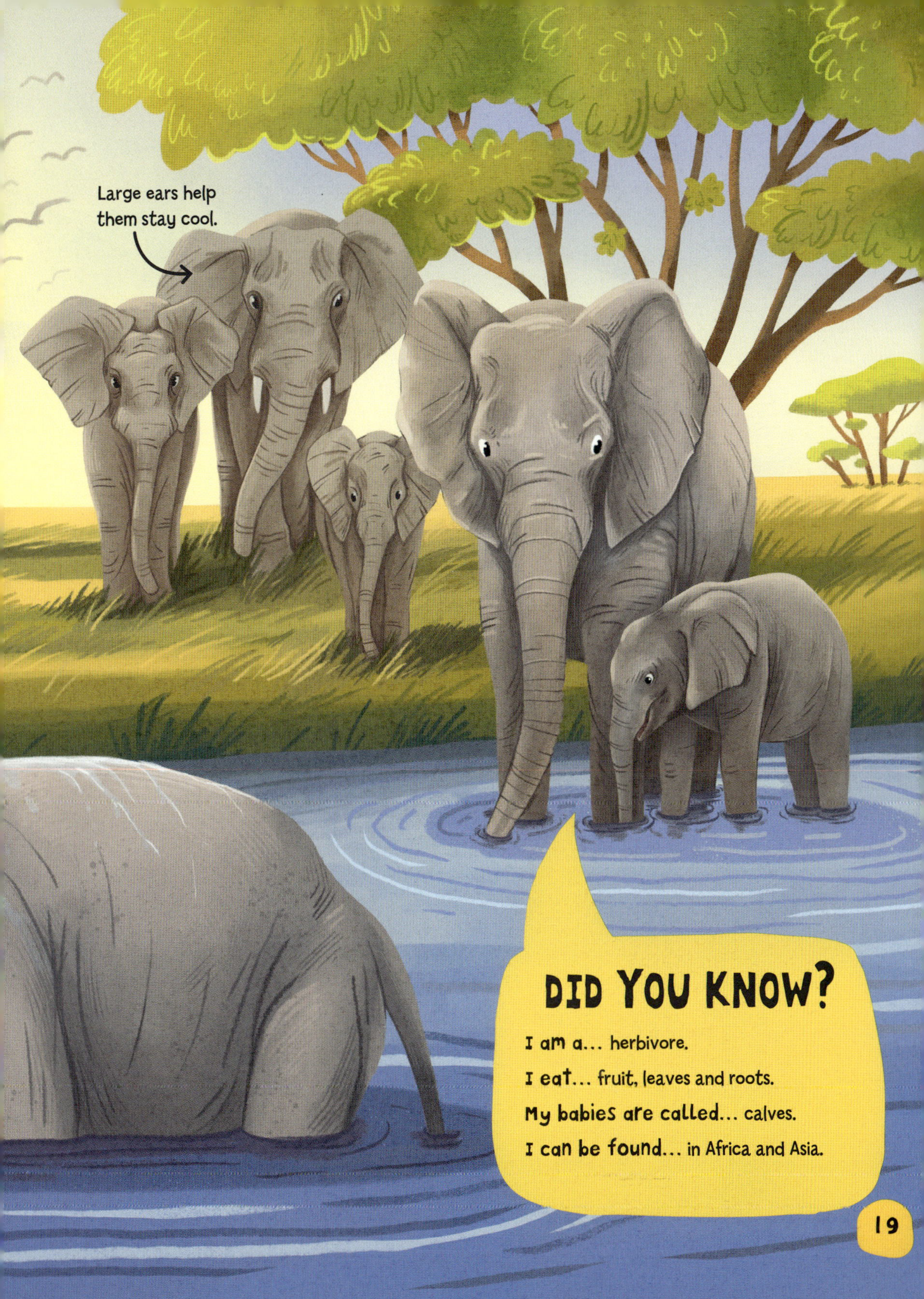
Large ears help them stay cool.
DID YOU KNOW?
I am a... herbivore.
I eat... fruit, leaves and roots.
My babies are called... calves.
I can be found... in Africa and Asia.

MORE GREAT MAMMALS

There are so many fascinating mammals around the world to learn about. How many of these animals have you seen in real life?

CAMEL

Camels can survive for long periods of time without drinking water because they don't sweat like humans do! That's very handy in their **desert** homes, where water is hard to find.

ARMADILLO

Armadillos are the only mammals that have hard shells! They are also one of the only **species** that can roll into a ball. This helps them stay safe from predators.

Armadillos can be found in Central and South America.
A great sense of smell helps them find fruit, insects and small animals to eat.
Armadillo babies are called pups.

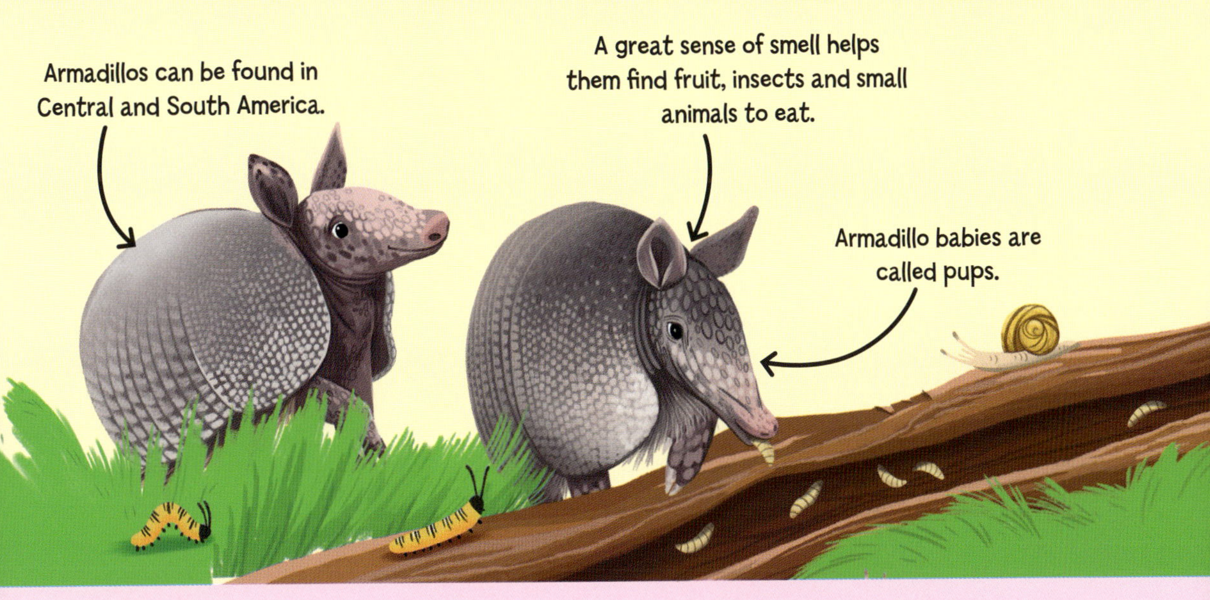

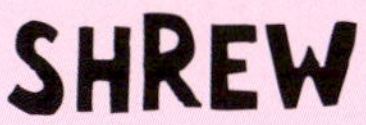

SHREW

Shrews are the smallest mammals of all! They look like mice, but have long, pointy snouts and usually live outdoors. They eat every 3-4 hours to stay warm and full of energy.

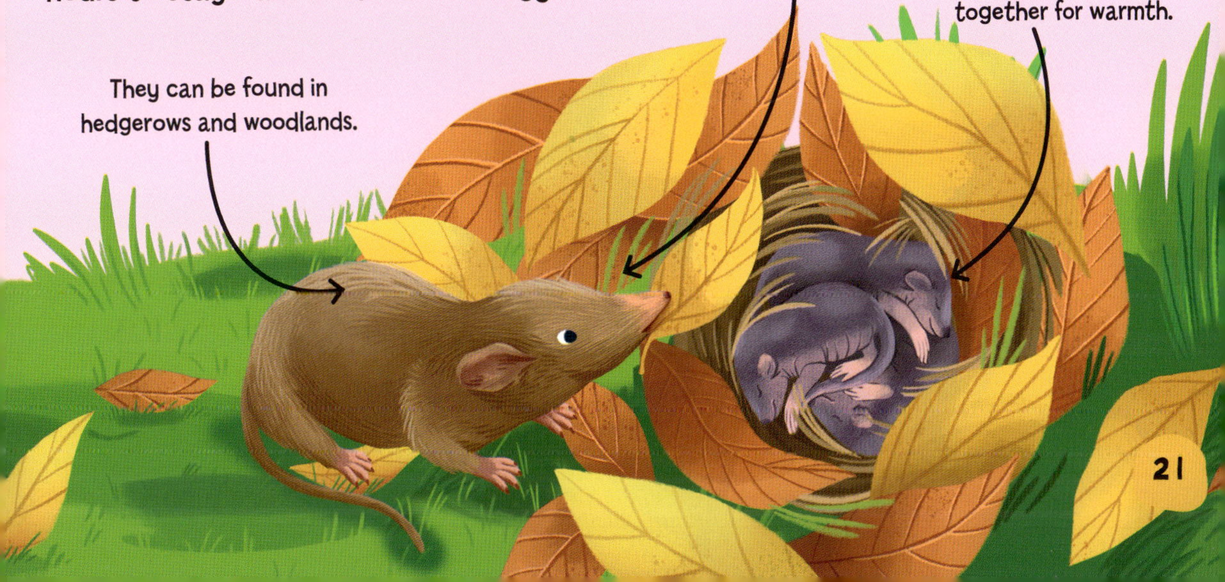
Shrews are omnivores and like to eat insects, seeds and **fungi**.
Baby shrews, called shrewlets, huddle together for warmth.
They can be found in hedgerows and woodlands.

NAME THAT MAMMAL

Can you work out which mammal each of these pictures are a part of? Clues have been provided for you based on facts from this book!

CLUE: This mammal lives in the Arctic.

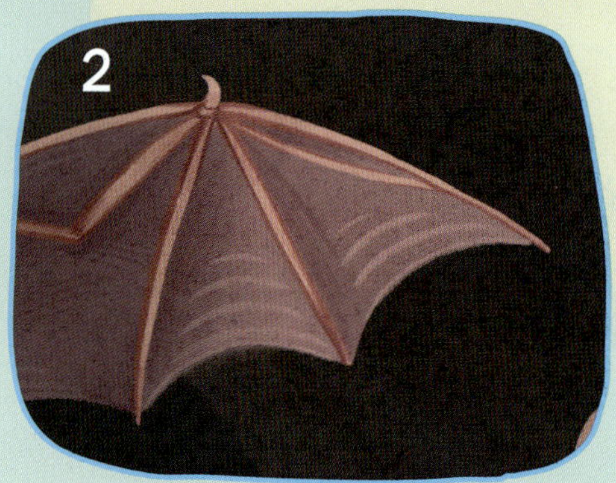

CLUE: This mammal can fly.

CLUE: This mammal is one of the biggest cats in the world!

CLUE: This mammal has a long trunk for smelling, drinking and picking up food.

CLUE: This mammal is most well known for its long neck.

CLUE: This mammal is the largest mammal in the world.

CLUE: This mammal can leap 30 feet (9 meters) in the air with one bounce!

DID YOU FIND THEM ALL?

Answers can be found on page 24.

GLOSSARY

Carnivore - an animal that mostly eats meat.

Desert - a place where it hardly ever rains.

Fungi - a group of living things that are neither plants or animals.

Echolocation - when animals use echoes from sound waves to move through their environment.

Grazing - to feed on growing grass.

Herbivore - an animal that only eats plants.

Nocturnal - an animal that sleeps during the day but becomes active during the night.

Omnivore - an animal that eats plants and meat, just like humans.

Predators - animals that hunt and kill other animals for food.

Prey - animals which are hunted by other animals as food.

Species - a group of living things that are the same as each other. For example, blue whales and humpback whales are different species.

Steering (verb) - to control direction.

Tusks - long, sharp pointed teeth.

Name That Mammal Answers:

1 - Polar Bear, 2 - Bat, 3 - Lion, 4 - Elephant, 5 - Giraffe, 6 - Blue Whale, 7 - Kangaroo.